# Songs of Milarepa

DOVER · THRIFT · EDITIONS

# Songs of Milarepa

## MILAREPA

DOVER PUBLICATIONS, INC.
Mineola, New York

# DOVER THRIFT EDITIONS

GENERAL EDITOR: PAUL NEGRI

EDITOR OF THIS VOLUME: RONALD HERDER

*Bibliographical Note*

This Dover edition, first published in 2003, is an unabridged republication of the work first published as *The Message of Milarepa* by John Murray, London, and Grove Press, Inc., New York, in 1958.

*Library of Congress Cataloging-in-Publication Data*

Mi-la-ras-pa, 1040-1123.
  [Message of Milarepa]
  Songs of Milarepa / Milarepa.
    p. cm.
  ISBN 0-486-42814-1 (pbk.)
  1. Tibetan poetry—Translations into English. I. Title.

PL3751.E3M48 2003
294.3'83—dc21

                                                  2002041719

Manufactured in the United States of America
Dover Publications, Inc., 31 East 2nd Street, Mineola, N.Y. 11501

*To*

*Gerard*

# Contents

[ix]

# Preface

Milarepa is the St Francis of Tibet. The accents of these songs are unmistakably those of the Fioretti; there is the same lyricism, the same tender sympathy, the same earthiness, for to the Cotton-clad as to the Poverello all nature was friend as well as chap-book. The difference is that the former learnt compassion through knowledge, whereas the latter found wisdom through love. Though far separated in space they were not in time, since the one lived on into the twelfth century, in which the other was born. The fame of each spread rapidly through his native land and has continued to this day: every Tibetan child knows the story of the great sinner who became the great sage, and his Life,* as chronicled by his favourite disciple Rechung, is a household favourite. In it we learn how, after his father's untimely death, he and his mother and sister were despoiled of their patrimony by his wicked uncle and aunt; how he ran away, for he was a boy of spirit, and learnt the black arts from a local sorcerer; conjured up a hailstorm which ruined their crops and caused the roof of their house to fall in and kill their guests at a harvest festival; how remorse overcame him for what he had done; how he then set out to find the truth and met his teacher Marpa; how Marpa, as penance, for seven years disciplined him savagely till

* *Tibet's Great Yogi Milarepa.* W. Y. Evans-Wentz. Oxford University Press, 1928; *Le Poète Tibétain Milarépa.* Jacques Bacot. Editions Bossard, 1925.

even his spirit was almost broken, but finally initiated him; how after long contemplation in his mountain solitudes he finally attained enlightenment and was consecrated by Marpa as his successor; and how he lived to a ripe old age, teaching the faith and working miracles, and died in the odour of sanctity.

Marpa his teacher was known as the Translator; though a Tibetan he had studied at the famous Indian University of Nalanda, become a proficient scholar of Sanskrit and translated many Buddhist works into his native tongue. While there he was the favourite disciple of Naropa, one of the most famous pandits of his day, and returned to Tibet determined to spread his master's teachings.

Naropa's was essentially a ritualist system based upon spells and diagrams (mantras and yantras), the power to use which could only be imparted directly from adept to disciple. Hence the name of his sect, the Kargyudpas, the followers of the oral tradition (it still flourishes today on the borders of Nepal and Sikkim and in Tibet proper). In order that the disciple may fit himself to receive this gift of power he must undergo prolonged intellectual study as well as a strenuous course of yogic exercises designed to produce the inner heat* and proof of success is the ability to withstand the extreme Himalayan cold wearing no more than a cotton loin-cloth; he is then entitled to the proud title of Repa, the cotton-clad, as Mila was. But this raising of the bodily temperature engenders such a flame of fervency in his mind that he is rapt to the contemplation of the suprasensual worlds.

* See *Tibetan Yoga and Secret Doctrines*. W. Y. Evans-Wentz. Oxford University Press, 1935.

Meanwhile control of the breath has enabled him to control the nervous energy and thereby the life-force and observe its manifestations on the subtle plane. Since the life-force is not mechanical, these manifestations appear to the mind of the meditator as gods and demons according to their gentleness or fierceness, and by the spells which he has learnt he can conjure them up, subject them to his will and reabsorb them. But he must not let himself be fascinated by his newly-won power, and here the guidance of the teacher is essential; by prolonged meditation upon the great symbol of the Void he must realize all these apparitions to be vacuous and undifferentiated and so attain experience of the ultimate, allowing enlightenment to arise spontaneously. Thereafter he is free to devote himself in compassion to the service of mankind.

Since the primitive religion of Tibet, Bon, was shamanistic and its world peopled by spirits, it is easy to understand the appeal to Tibetans of a Buddhism so much akin to their own belief. The teachers of the ritualist Orders, beginning with Padma Sambhava, had only to possess power and knowledge superior to that of the Bon shamans to convert the superstitious populace. And so it was that Buddhism gained the whole country in a short space of time.

Milarepa's part in this is recorded in two books: his Life and his Songs. In the latter work an account of the most important events in his spiritual career serves to frame the songs themselves, for upon each occasion he expresses his deepest thoughts in song, the accents of which range from the lyrical to the mystic and high philosophic. Those in the present volume, which are only a small fraction of the vast number in the original work, have been carefully selected to show every facet of his teaching. Only a few of them have ever been translated and these are not readily available to the public. The style adopted in this translation is deliberately archaic in order to give the same impression that the language of the songs themselves does to the Tibetan of today. But more than literal translation is necessary: there must be a certain adaptation in order to make comprehensible to the Western reader the subtleties of this highly intricate form of Buddhism with its unfamiliar technical terms, yet this with due knowledge of the indigenous traditions and respect for them. Many of the poems are deceptively simple and upon more mature consideration will be found to enshrine profound spiritual truths. And though the paths of Milarepa and St Francis separate, who is to say that they do not ultimately converge?

I wish to express my thanks to the Rani Dorji and her mentor, Kung Kusho, who have been kind enough to revise this translation.

The text is that of the Pekin Edition from the Rockhill Collection in the Library of Congress. The Tibetan names have been phonetically and not literally transcribed.

A glossary of some technical terms is appended, to which the numbers in the text refer. It would be deceptive to try to enlarge upon them within the limited scope of this book. Those who are interested may refer to the Tibetan texts given in translation in the above-mentioned works of Dr Evans-Wentz to carry their interpretation a stage further, though they should be chary of accepting the whole of his commentary as faithfully reflecting the original tradition. But a full understanding of them no book can give; it requires a life-time of continual application.

H.C.

*Cala d'Or, Majorca*
*September,* 1958

# The Quest of Milarepa

*When named I am the man apart;*
*I am the sage of Tibet;*
*I am Milarepa.*
*I hear little but counsel much;*
*I reflect little but persevere much;*
*I sleep little but endure in meditation much.*
*Knowing one thing I have experience of all things;*
*knowing all things I comprehend them to be one;*
*I have experience of true reality.*
*My narrow bed gives me ease to stretch and bend;*
*my thin clothing makes my body warm;*
*my scanty fare satisfies my belly.*
*I am the goal of every great meditator;*
*I am the meeting place of the faithful;*
*I am the coil of birth and death and decay.*
*I have no preference for any country;*
*I have no home in any place;*
*I have no store of provisions for my livelihood.*
*I have no fondness for material things;*
*I make no distinction between clean and unclean in food;*
*I have little torment of suffering.*
*I have little desire for self-esteem;*
*I have little attachment or bias;*
*I have found the freedom of Nirvana.*
*I am the comforter of the aged;*

*I am the playmate of children;*
*the sage, I wander through the kingdoms of the world.*
*I pray that ye men and gods may dwell at ease.*

2

Obeisance to their lordships the teachers.
Especially do I pray them of their grace to be my refuge.
When ye look at me I am an idle, idle man;
when I look at myself I am a busy, busy man.
Since upon the plain of uncreated infinity
I am building, building the tower of ecstasy,
I have no time for building houses.
Since upon the steppe of the void of truth
I am breaking, breaking the savage fetter of suffering,
I have no time for ploughing family land.
Since at the bourn of unity ineffable
I am subduing, subduing the demon-foe of self,
I have no time for subduing angry foe-men.
Since in the palace of mind which transcends duality
I am waiting, waiting for spiritual experience as my bride,
I have no time for setting up house.
Since in the circle of the Buddhas of my body
I am fostering, fostering the child of wisdom,
I have no time for fostering snivelling children.
Since in the frame of the body, the seat of all delight,
I am saving, saving precious instruction and reflection,
I have no time for saving wordly wealth.
Since upon the mountain of limitless truth
I am tending, tending the wild-horse of self-knowledge,
I have no time for tending sheep.

Since out of the clay of flesh and bones
I am building, building up the miraculous reliquary,
I have no time for moulding sacred images.
Since upon the apex of the triangle of my heart
I am raising, raising the butter-flame of clear light,
I have no time for offering the sacred fire.
Since in the temple of the undifferentiated void of bliss,
before the image of the tranquillized mind,
I am offering, offering perpetual oblations,
I have no time for formal worshipping.
Since upon the sheet of pure mind
I am writing, writing desireless characters,
I have no time for painting sacred pictures.
Since in the skull-cup of the very void
I am churning, churning the poison of the passions,
I have no time for churning holy butter.
Since in the close retreat of good intent
I am cherishing, cherishing as friends
the sentient beings of the six kinds,[1]
I have no time for cherishing kinsfolk.
Since in the presence of the fathers, the teachers,
I am burdening, burdening my soul with counsel
I have no time for growing old in ordinary ploys.
Since in the solitude of the mountain-cell
I am perfecting, perfecting my heart's illumination
I have no time for yielding to sleep's oblivion.
Since from the conch of my mouth triangular
I am singing, singing the song of spirituality,
I have no time for making leisured conversation.

3

Obeisance to the fathers, the teachers.
The impartial mountain
is my sage's monastery.
The men and women almsgivers of the kingdom
are the providers of my sage's food.
I thought, I the sage shall go to dwell
in the monastery of the uninhabited mountains.
This counsel enjoined by the teacher,
if borne, is lighter than a feather;
if concealed, is more delectable than precious gold;
if practised in contrition and fear, is stronger than a fortress.
I the sage am a lion among men.
Three winters have I delighted in the deep forests;
three summers have I delighted in the snow-peaks;
three springs have I delighted in the alpine meadows;
three autumns have I sought alms of whatever sort.
My mind has delighted in my teacher's counsel;
my mouth has delighted in singing songs of my soul;
my body has delighted in a cotton cloth from Nepal.
I have lived delighting, thus delighting.
Do ye also live rejoicing, thus rejoicing.

## 4

When the tiger-year was ending
and the hare-year beginning
on the sixth day of the month of the barking of the fox,*
I grew weary of the things of this world;
and in my yearning for solitude
I came to the sanctuary wilderness, Mount Everest.
Then heaven and earth took counsel together
and sent forth the whirlwind as messenger.
The elements of wind and water seethed
and the dark clouds of the south rolled up in concert;
the peerless twain, sun and moon, were made prisoner
and the twenty-eight constellations of the moon were fastened
    together;
the eight planets in their courses were cast into chains
and the faint milky way was delivered into bondage;
the little stars were altogether shrouded in mist
and when all things were covered in the complexion of mist
for nine days and nine nights the snow fell,
steadily throughout the eighteen times of day and night it fell.
When it fell heavily the flakes were as big as the flock of wool,
and fell floating like feathered birds.
When the snow fell lightly the flakes were small as spindles,
and fell circling like bees.

    * The Tibetan calendar is based upon a twelve-year cycle, each
year named after an animal; the twelve months are similarly named.

*Again, they were as small as peas or mustard-seed,*
*and fell turning like distaffs.*
*Moreover the snow surpassed measure in depth,*
*the peak of white snow above reached to the heavens*
*and the trees of the forest below were bowed down.*
*The dark hills were clad in white,*
*ice formed upon the billowing lakes*
*and the blue Tsangpo\* was constrained in its depths.*
*The earth became like a plain without hill or valley,*
*and in natural consequence of such a great fall*
*the lay folk were mewed up;*
*famine overtook the four-footed cattle,*
*and the small deer especially found no food;*
*the feathered birds above lacked nourishment,*
*and the marmots and field-mice below hid in their burrows;*
*the jaws of beasts of prey were stiffened together.*
*In such fearsome circumstances*
*this strange fate befell me, Milarepa.*
*There were these three: the snowstorm driving down from on*
  *high,*
*the icy blast of mid-winter,*
*and the cotton cloth which I, the sage Mila, wore;*
*and between them rose a contest on that white snow peak.*
*The falling snow melted into goodly water;*
*the wind, though rushing mightily, abated of itself,*
*and the cotton cloth blazed like fire.*
*Life and death wrestled there after the fashion of champions,*
*and swords crossed victorious blades.*
*That I won there the heroic fight*
*will be an example to all the faithful*

\* The Brahmaputra.

and a true example to all great contemplatives;
more especially will it prove the greater excellence
of the single cotton cloth and the inner heat.
For all hidden causes of disorder were balanced
and henceforth, inward and outward conflict past, were
    reconciled.
The two breaths, both the hot and the cold,
imparted their invigoration
and I utterly overcame the snow-faced demon,
who promised to obey my commands thereafter.
Then I ordered all aright in stillness
and, without seeking to summon the legions of this world,
as sage was victor in the strife that day.
For I am of my grandfather and wear the tiger skin:
when I put on the fox skin there was none to say me nay.
I am my father's son and of the race of champions:
I never suffered defeat from an angry foe.
I am of the breed of the lion the king of beasts:
I never dwelt but in the heart of the snows.
Therefore the foe's preparation proved vanity.

If ye steadfastly obey the words of this old man
the teaching of the practice of conjuration
will spread hereafter and many saints will arise;
and I, Milarepa the sage, shall be most famous
throughout the kingdoms of the world.
Ye, disciples, recollected, will be full of faith
and your good report will be noised abroad.

Mount Tisé and Lake Mapang at its foot (better known as Mt Kailas and Lake Manasrowar) were originally the holy places of Bon. Milarepa, however, having proved the master of the Bon priests in magic, drove them thence and took possession in the name of Buddhism. To this day they comprise one of the most important Buddhist pilgrimages, where many yogis live and which multitudes of pilgrims visit every year. This is Milarepa's song of triumph.

5

*That the white ice-peak of Tisé, great in fame,*
*is just a mountain covered with snow,*
*proves the whiteness of Buddha's teaching.*
*That the turquoise lake of Mapang, great in fame,*
*is water through which water flows,*
*proves the dissolution of all created things.*
*That I, Milarepa, great in fame,*
*am an old and naked man,*
*proves that I have forsaken and set at nought self-interest.*
*That I am a singer of little songs,*
*proves that I have learnt to read the world as a book.*
*That I grasp a staff in my hand,*
*proves that I have forded the sea of transmigration.*
*Since I have power over both appearance and mind,*
*when I perform mighty magic feats,*
*I depend not upon the gods of this world.*
*This Tisé, prince among mountains on earth,*
*is a mighty power to all followers of the Buddha,*
*and a mighty power to Mila the Kargyudpa especially.*

# The Sage

## 6

I, who am the master revered,
wandered in the illusory city of the six kinds of beings[1]
like a small child whose impressions are illusory
and underwent manifold illusions of activity.

Sometimes the illusion of hunger arose
and I ate as food alms of whatever sort.
Sometimes I gnawed at stones for discipline,
sometimes I fed upon the void,
and sometimes I inured myself to hardship as a substitute.

Sometimes the illusion of thirst arose
and I drank the cool blue water of the slate rocks.
Sometimes I partook of my own water,
sometimes I drank from the stream of compassion,
and sometimes I drank magic from the sky-travelling goddess.*

Sometimes the illusion of freezing arose
and I clad myself in a single cotton cloth.
Sometimes I glowed with the blissful inner heat,
sometimes I inured myself to hardship as a substitute.

Sometimes the illusion of friendship arose,
and I trusted in knowledge and wisdom as friends.
I practised the ten holy virtues,[2]

* See introduction to song 27, p. 44.

*I made experience of trascendent contemplation,*
*and I thoroughly examined the self-knowing mind.*

*I, the sage, am the lion among men,*
*who has spread out the turquoise mane of contemplation*
*and possessed of the teeth and claws of meditation*
*among the snow peaks has devoted himself to experiment*
*and hopes as fruit to attain virtue.*

*I, the sage, am the tiger among men,*
*who has perfected the three powers of enlightened mind.*[3]
*With the smile of inseparable method and wisdom*
*he has dwelt in the healing forest of clear light*
*and hopes to attain his neighbour's good as fruit.*

*I, the sage, am the vulture among men,*
*who has spread the wings of the bright ritual of creation*
*and with the flapping pinions of the ritual of perfection*[4]
*has wheeled in the sky of transcendent union with truth.*
*I have rested upon the rock of absolute reality*
*and hope to effect the twofold good*
*of my neighbour and myself as fruit.*

*I, the sage, am the holy one among men.*
*I am Milarepa.*
*I am he who goes his own way;*
*I am he who has counsel for every circumstance;*
*I am the sage who has no fixed abode.*
*I am he who is unaffected whatever befall;*
*I am the alms-seeker who has no food;*
*I am the naked man who has no clothes;*
*I am the beggar who has no possessions.*
*I am he who takes no thought for the morrow;*

## THE SAGE

*I am he who has no house here nor dwelling there;*
*I am the victor who has known consummation.*
*I am the madman who counts death happiness;*
*I am he who has naught and needs naught.*

7

Teacher, counsel and disciple are three;
zeal, endurance and faith are three;
wisdom, mercy and beatific vision are three;
and these are the everlasting guides.

This noiseless solitude
is the guide to long-held contemplation.

The sainted teacher Jetsun
is the guide to lighten darkness.

His unwearying faith
is the guide to felicity.

The discernment of the five senses
is the guide that frees from the thrall of sentience.

The precept of the teacher of the Kargyudpa Order
is the guide to show forth the triple body.[5]

This triple jewel and place of refuge
is the guide to infallibility.

Led by these six guides
the sage goes to the plain of great bliss
and dwells in the state of no difference nor distinction
and rejoices in his proper station of self-knowledge and
    self-deliverance.

## THE SAGE

For he has firmly established himself
in the understanding of truth and reality,
and in the desert where no man comes
the sage sings this song of joy in a voice of thunder;
a pleasant rain falls in every quarter
and the flower of mercy puts forth its petals;
the fruit of illumination ripens in purity
and the virtue of enlightenment fills everything.

## 8

Obeisance to my father, the jewel that fulfils my every desire.
May he grant of his grace that his son may meet with assistance
and in my own body, the habitation of the godhead,
make me welcome the knowledge of reality, I pray.

In fear of death I built a house,
and my house is the house of the void of truth;
now I fear not death.

In fear of cold I sought a coat,
and my coat is the coat of the inner heat;
now I fear not cold.

In fear of want I sought wealth,
and my wealth is glorious, unending, sevenfold;
now I fear not want.

In fear of hunger I sought food,
and my food is the food of meditation upon truth;
now I fear not hunger.

In fear of thirst I sought drink,
and my drink is the nectar of right knowledge;
now I fear not thirst.

In fear of weariness I sought a companion,
and my companion is the everlasting void of bliss;
now I fear not weariness.

THE SAGE

*In fear of error I sought a path,*
*and my path is the path of transcendent union;*
*now I fear not error.*

*I am a sage who possesses in plentitude*
*the manifold treasures of desire*
*and wherever I dwell I am happy.*

*The lion stronghold of the tiger cave of Yolmo*
*has affection for the tiger's loud roar,*
*and this has irresistibly constrained me to retreat.*

*The moaning of the tiger-cub rouses compassion,*
*irresistibly constraining me*
*to meditation upon enlightenment.*

*The chatter of the monkey enchains the attention,*
*irresistibly constraining me*
*to upwelling of world-weariness.*

*The shrill cry of the young monkey moves the heart to laughter,*
*irresistibly constraining me*
*to meditation upon the quickening of the mind.*

*The plaint of the cuckoo grieves the innermost soul,*
*irresistibly constraining me to shedding of tears.*

*The song of the lark enchants the ear,*
*irresistibly constraining me to sweet listening.*

*The busy cawing of the raven,*
*the companion of the sage, benefits the intelligence.*

*He who dwells in such places rejoices in spirit
and if he is companionless is glad thereof.*

*May this inspired song of the sage's joy
take away the suffering of mankind.*

# 9

As happy as a layman delivered from a pit,
so is the sage when he has renounced his inheritance.
As happy as a good horse freed from his halter,
so is the sage when he has transcended partiality.
As happy as a beast dwelling unwounded,
so is the sage who dwells alone.
As happy as the eagle flying high in the firmament,
so is the sage who is settled, contemplating.
As happy as the icy wind rushing through the air,
so is the sage whose path is unhindered.
As happy as the shepherd keeping blessed white sheep,
so is the sage who keeps the clear void of mind.
As happy as princely mount Meru in the centre of the universe,
so is the sage who is immutable.
As happy as the stream of a great river,
so is the sage who enjoys the stream of thought.
As happy as the corpse in a cemetery,
so is the sage who forsakes this world's affairs.
As happy as the stone cast into the sea,
so is the sage who will not return.
As happy as the sun rising in the heavens,
so is the sage whose light shines for all.
As happy as the leaf plucked from the plane tree,
so is the sage who will not be born again.
This is the song of the sage's twelve happinesses;
may all of you quicken the faith and practise it.

*10*

Ye kings and ministers who desire happiness,
if ye had the kingship of Milarepa
and kept it, ye would be altogether happy
both in this life and hereafter.
The kingship of Mila is on this wise.
The precious wheel of the faith
brings practise of virtue throughout day and night.
The precious jewel of wisdom
fulfils the duty of all, to self and neighbour.
The precious spouse of the moral law
is adorned with ornaments of surpassing beauty.
The precious minister of deep meditation
stores up two-fold wealth of merit and wisdom.
The precious elephant of chastity
bears the heavy burden of the teaching of Buddha.
The precious thoroughbred of perseverance
guides to the place without sin or self.
The precious jewel of instruction and reflection
overcomes the enemy of false discernment.
If ye had this kingship
ye would be the most eminent and famous of kings;
ye would always vanquish hostile factions;
ye would make your subjects undertake all virtuous works.
May all sentient beings, who in former lives have begotten me,
accomplish my kingly commandment.

# Renunciation

## *11*

Obeisance to the excellent lord my teacher.

Wealth is like the dew on a blade of grass,
so give alms without covetousness.

When thou hast obtained the substantial blessings of humanity,
keep the commandments as the apple of thine eye.

Anger is the root of damnation,
so though thy life be forfeit meditate upon patience.

Be not idle in bettering thy neighbour and thyself,
but show zeal in works of virtue.

In thine error the Great Vehicle* has no meaning for thee,
so meditate its meaning in singleness of mind.

When thou hast sought the Buddha and found him not,
contemplate the essence of thine own mind.
Faith is like the mist of autumn,
so when it vanishes pray for steadfastness.

* See introduction to song 26, p. 42.

*12*

*Obeisance to gracious Marpa.*

To be resolved to abandon selfishness is joy.
To renounce the love of home is joy.
To be free from the village magistrate is joy.
To make no theft of the common store is joy.
Not to hanker for a householder's estate is joy.
Not to have a reason for covetousness is joy.
To be rich in spiritual wealth is joy.
To ignore the misery of gaining a livelihood is joy.
To have no fear of loss or diminution is joy.
To be unafraid of corruption is joy.
To have assurance deep within the heart is joy.
To be untrammelled by the almsgiver's self-interest is joy.
To be unwearying in help is joy.
To live without hypocrisy is joy.
To walk in the faith in every deed is joy.
To be untired by a fondness for journeying is joy.
To have no fear of sudden death is joy.
To be unafraid of robbery is joy.
To meet furtherance of holiness is joy.
To shun evil deeds is joy.
To be diligent in works of piety is joy.
To have done with the harmful spirit of anger is joy.
To eschew pride and envy is joy.

# RENUNCIATION

*To see the eight wordly principles[6] as sinful is joy.*
*To abandon them with equanimity is joy.*
*To be free from hope and fear is joy.*
*In the sphere of the incomprehensible clear light is joy.*
*In the realm of the undiscriminated wisdom is joy.*
*In the state of the self-created primordial being is joy.*
*To have ordered the mind and senses aright is joy.*
*To have purified the intelligence that governs action is joy.*
*To stop the coming and going of the imagination is joy.*

*These are my manifold kinds of joy*
*and this is the sage's song of happiness*
*and I pray for no other bliss.*
*For death is joy if thou do no evil,*
*and life is joy if thou increase thy piety.*
*Food and clothing are the almsgivers' care,*
*but this is the most precious teacher's grace*
*and is the measure of the sage's joy.*

*13*

*The way of the world is illusion:*
*I strive after true reality.*
*To be moved by earthly possessions is illusion:*
*I endeavour to rise above duality.*
*To be the world's servant is illusion:*
*I wander in the mountains alone.*
*Wealth and possessions are illusion:*
*I renounce for the sake of the faith any I may have.*
*External things are illusion:*
*I contemplate the mind.*
*Distinctive thought is illusion:*
*I follow after sapience.*
*Conditional truth is illusion:*
*I dispose the absolute truth.*
*The printed book is illusion:*
*I meditate upon the counsels of the ear-whispered tradition.*
*Philosophical argument is illusion:*
*I study at length that which is unfeigned.*
*Both birth and death are illusion:*
*I contemplate the deathless truth.*
*Ordinary knowledge is illusion:*
*I exercise myself in wisdom.*
*The delight of mental thought is illusion:*
*I dwell in the state of reality.*

## 14

When I am in the presence of my teacher
a mental state like a well-tempered sword arises
and my soul rejoices to have resolved all inner doubts.
When I am in the midst of the multitude
a mental state like a lighted lamp arises
and my soul rejoices to explain the spiritual exhortations.
When I am upon the peak of Gangkar
a mental state like a roaring white lion arises
and my soul rejoices to defeat my opponents in argument.
When I am upon the side of Drakmar
a mental state like a lordly vulture arises
and my soul rejoices to still the waves of the ocean of outward sense.
When I wander through countries impartially
a mental state like a striped young tiger arises
and my soul rejoices to have no desire for feeling.
When I am within the round of transmigration
a mental state like a lotus flower arises
and my soul rejoices to be stripped of worldly sin.
When I am in the throng of worldly men
a mental state like shining quicksilver arises
and my soul rejoices to be naked of perception.
When I am among the faithful hearers
a mental state like the mind of the reverend Mila arises
and my soul rejoices to pour forth counsels in song.
My rejoicing is due to my teacher's grace
and this heart unfeigned is the earnest of Buddhahood.

*15*

My son, as monastery be content with the body
for the bodily substance is the palace of divinity.
As teacher be content with the mind
for knowledge of the truth is the beginning of holiness.
As book be content with outward things
for their number is a symbol of the way of deliverance.
As food be content to feed on ecstasy
for stillness is the perfect likeness of divinity.
As clothing be content to put on the inner heat
for the sky-travelling goddesses wear the warmth of bliss.
Companions be content to forsake
for solitude is president of the divine assembly.
Raging enemies be content to shun
for enmity is a traveller upon the wrong path.
With demons be content to meditate upon the Void
for magic apparitions are creations of the mind.

## 16

He who is not eloquent in speech
may or may not have the gift of preaching.
Though this present suppliant have it not, his intention is good.
All religious teachings are comprised in these six sublime virtues.

Charity is the royal religious quality:
if a man gives away all that he has
he will receive the kingdom of the most high god.
Charity gladdens the hearts of the followers of the faith.

Morality is the chief ladder to freedom:
no monk who has entered the religion of Buddha
can ever dispense with it.
Lay hold on this truth, O ye assembled here.

Patience is the saintly religious quality:
every follower of Shakya Muni
clothes himself fitly in the blessedness of patience,
raiment which it is hard to wear.

Perseverance is the short road to freedom:
it is the necessary road to all holiness.
He who lacks it is bereft of hope.
A man must mount the steed of perseverance.
No one who has heard and deeply pondered
on the acquiring of merit by the practice of religion
can ever dispense with it.

Meditation is the religious quality that brings knowledge.
It is close retreat to gain double merit.
Since it is surely needful to abide in close retreat
this is the cure for distraction.
I pray you all to apply yourselves
to winning your own and your neighbour's good.

Wisdom is the religious quality which looks to true reality.
It is the sole treasury of every Buddha,
the mine of inexhaustible delights to those who find it,
the wealth that relieves the poverty of all mankind.
It completely removes the eight impediments[7]
and confers the highest blessedness.
He who gathers knowledge is precious
and gradually achieves authority.

## 17

Alas for the sentient beings of the world:
the shadow of evil deeds is black darkness;
the thieves of distinctive thought, cruel in their multitude;
it is a great effort to pursue the jewel of concentration;
it is meet to keep watch undistractedly;
the wicked man has no thought of death's coming.
You and I, Rechung, together must go
to the snows of the Himalaya.

The stream of the world is a long path above the abyss;
the robbers of the five senses, savage in their turbulence;
it is a great effort to grasp the child of knowledge;
it is meet to seek the guidance of wisdom;
the wicked man has no thought of death's coming.
You and I, Rechung, together must go
to the snows of the Himalaya.

The mountain of sin is a lofty peak;
the huntsman of suffering, hot in pursuit with his hounds;
it is a great effort to kill the deer of ecstasy;
it is meet to flee to the goal of reality;
The wicked man has no thought of death's coming.
You and I, Rechung, together must go
to the snows of the Himalaya.

Upon the ruined house of the illusory body
the rain of days and hours falls
and the drops of the years and months beat down.
It is a great effort to destroy the body's ruin;
it is meet to use the downpour of readiness to die;
the wicked man has no thought of death's coming.
You and I, Rechung, together must go
to the snows of the Himalaya.

The ocean of the world is a profound depth;
it is meet that the child of knowledge should swim.
It is a great effort to move against the waves of illusion;
it is meet to go to the island of immanence;
the wicked man has no thought of death's coming.
You and I, Rechung, together must go
to the snows of the Himalaya.

The meadow of amorous dalliance is a broad expanse;
the mire of marriage, a profound depth;
it is a great effort to revive the ox of aversion;
it is meet to pursue meditation upon freedom;
the wicked man has no thought of death's coming.
You and I, Rechung, together must go
to the snows of the Himalaya.

# Occasional Wisdom

## 18

At first a wife is a goddess wreathed in smiles
and her husband never tires of gazing at her face.
She soon becomes a fiend with corpse-like eyes;
if he casts a reproach at her she gives two in return;
if he takes her by the hair she has him by the leg;
if he strikes her with a stick she beats him with a ladle.
In the end she becomes a toothless old hag
and her fiendish look of anger prays upon the mind.
I have renounced such a devilish scold
and I do not want a maiden bride.

*19*

At first a son is as pleasing as a scion of the gods,
irresistible to the loving heart.
He is soon relentlessly hounded for debt,
though his parents give their all he is never content.
He brings home the daughter of some strange man
and turns outside his kindly father and mother.
Though his father calls he gives no answer,
though his mother cries out he speaks never a word.
At last he becomes a hasty-tempered lodger
and drives them away with false complaints.
Now this foe sprung of their loins
preys continually upon their minds.
I have renounced such worldly swill,
and I do not want a son.

## 20

*O precious trinity divine, be my refuge.**
*O teacher, grant me grace I pray.*

*Ye worldly spiritual counsellors*
*who have not converted your own mind within,*
*how can ye convert passionate mortals without?*

*Arbours with white peacocks spreading their tails*
*are like lightning that illumines for an instant.*
*Bethink ye, are ye not counsellors of this sort?*

*Tea in a monastery above the village*
*is like self-deceit that provokes calamity.*
*Bethink ye, are ye not counsellors of this sort?*

*The bustle of laymen*
*is like an angry foe attacking in the rear.*
*Bethink ye, are ye not counsellors of this sort?*

*Horses, wealth and sheep, these three supports of life,*
*are like a storm-wind bending the tops of the grass.*
*Bethink ye, are ye not counsellors of this sort?*

*This illusory body compact of suffering*
*is like a gilded corpse.*
*Bethink ye, are ye not counsellors of this sort?*

* See introduction to poem 37, p. 66.

[32]

This presiding over chapters of reverend nuns
is like the company of peasants for lack of gentry.
Bethink ye, are ye not counsellors of this sort?

This multitude desirous of food
is like confiscation by post-service and taxes.
Bethink ye, are ye not counsellors of this sort?

This soothsaying, sorcery, and astrology, this triple charlatanry
is like a liar's disputatiousness.
Bethink ye, are ye not counsellors of this sort?

This little song of yours that deceives your hearers
is like the purring of a wicked cat.
Bethink ye, are ye not counsellors of this sort?

This lordship of a patrimony of house and lands
is like eagerness to court a simpleton.
Bethink ye, are ye not counsellors of this sort?

This lively gathering of disciples
is like a nobleman's retinue.
Bethink ye, are ye not counsellors of this sort?

This teaching of the faith without its meaning
is like an impostor's mendacity.
Bethink ye, are ye not counsellors of this sort?

He who in his husbandry seeks not his own profit
but the profit of his neighbour is the virtuous man.

*21*

The next three poems relate to a single episode. One day when Milarepa is in one of his hermitages meditating, a hunted stag seeks refuge with him. It is shortly followed by a hound in hot pursuit. Finally the hunter arrives, bow in hand, but to his surprise finds the stag lying peacefully to one side of Milarepa and the hound to the other, for Milarepa by singing the first of these songs has softened the hound's heart. The hunter is so impressed that he too is converted and in the second song offers Milarepa the life of the stag and all that he has and begs for spiritual guidance. This Milarepa gives him in the third song. He eventually forsakes the world and becomes one of Milarepa's disciples.

*I bow at the feet of lord Marpa of Lhobrak.*
*May he grant of his grace that the anger of sentient things be*
*    stilled.*
*Thou creature that hast a dog's body and a wolf's countenance,*
*thou of the dog's body and wolf's countenance, hearken to*
*    Mila's song.*
*Since thou considerest an enemy whatever thou seest*
*thy mind is fevered with the evil thought of anger.*
*Thou wast born in the body of a wicked dog*
*and dwellest in a state of misery and hunger;*
*there is no stilling the pangs of thy suffering.*
*If thou hast not grasped the form of thine own inward mind*
*what profits it thee to grasp the outward body of another?*
*The time has come that thou grasp thine own mind.*
*Renounce the heart of anger and abide here.*

*According to thy present thought,*
*devoured by intolerable suffering and danger,*
*thou fearest lest the stag escape thee on the side of yonder*
*    mountain,*
*hoping to grasp it on the side of this one nearby.*
*Torn between hope and fear thou wanderest through the world.*
*I will give thee instruction in the six doctrines of Naropa,*[8]
*and show thee the meditation upon the great symbol of the*
*    Void.*

## 22

This black stag upon my right hand adorned with conch-white
    antlers,
if I slay it, will satisfy my appetite for seven days.
This which I the mortal need not, I offer, O teacher.
I pray thee lead this black stag into the way of great bliss;
this bitch Red Lightning into the way of enlightenment;
and Gonpodorje into the way of liberation.

This bitch Red Lightning on my left hand,
if I loose it, will catch even the fowls of the air.
This which I the mortal need not, I offer, O teacher.
I pray thee lead this black stag into the place of great bliss;
this bitch Red Lightning into the way of enlightenment;
and Gonpodorje into the way of liberation.

This black lasso adorned with a ring at the end,
if I use it, will capture even the yak from the north.
This which I the mortal need not, I offer, O teacher.
I pray thee lead this black stag into the place of great bliss;
this bitch Red Lightning into the way of enlightenment;
and Gonpodorje into the way of liberation.

This hunter's coat of antelope-skin trimmed with dyed goat-skin,
if I put it on, will give warmth even on the white snow mountains.
This which I the mortal need not, I offer, O teacher.

*I pray thee lead this black stag into the place of great bliss;
this bitch Red Lightning into the place of enlightenment;
and Gonpodorje into the place of liberation.*

*This slender arrow grasped in my right hand,
adorned with four feathers and a vermilion tip,
if I loose it, will pierce whatever it strikes.
This which I the mortal need not, I offer, O teacher.
I pray thee lead this black stag into the place of great bliss;
this bitch Red Lightning into the place of enlightenment;
and Gonpodorje into the place of liberation.*

*This excellent white bow grasped in my left hand,
adorned with birch-bark and a Chinese bow-string,
if I loose it, will thunder like the dragon of the sky.
This which I the mortal need not, I offer, O teacher.
I pray thee lead this black stag into the way of great bliss;
this bitch Red Lightning into the place of enlightenment;
and Gonpodorje into the place of liberation.*

## 23

Hearken now and list to me, O hunter.
Though great the noise of thunder, it is but an empty sound;
though beautiful the rainbow hues they vanish and are gone;
though the world delights the mind it is but a dream.
Though the objects of desire bring great joy
they are the cause of folly;
though the concrete seems permanent it swiftly is dissolved.
That which yesterday existed does not exist today;
the man who lived last year, this year is dead.
He who was a staunch friend becomes an enemy;
the food which was good to eat turns poisonous;
he who was grateful for kindness becomes insolent;
he who did evil to others harms himself.
Among a hundred heads thine own head is dear to thee;
any of thy fingers when severed causes pain;
among a numerous household thou lovest thyself.
The time has come for thee to raise thine head in independence;
this fleeting life swiftly vanishes;
it is not meet to put off practice of the faith.
Loving kinsfolk cast thee into this world's round;
the time has now come to rely upon a teacher.
Happiness in this life brings bliss in the next;
to practise holy faith the time has come.

Rechung, Milarepa's favourite disciple, has at last
received the master's permission to set off on a
missionary journey to Ü, the central province of
Tibet in which Lhasa is situated. In this poem *24*
Milarepa gives him his final counsels and his
blessing. In the next he laments his departure.

*O teacher, my son, wilt thou depart to Ü or wilt thou not?*
*Teacher, if thou depart to Ü*
*sometimes thou shalt have visions of food.*
*When thou hast these visions of food*
*eat the food of inexhaustible ecstasy,*
*realize that all sweet things are illusory*
*and consider all appearance as the body of truth.*

*Sometimes thou shalt have visions of clothing.*
*When thou hast these visions of clothing*
*put on the clothing of the heat of inward bliss,*
*realize that all soft things are illusory*
*and consider all appearance as the body of truth.*

*Sometimes thou shalt have visions of thy home.*
*When thou hast these visions of thy home*
*make thy home the abiding home of the truth,*
*realize that all paternal homes are illusory*
*and consider all appearance as the body of truth.*

*Sometimes thou shalt have visions of wealth.*
*When thou hast these visions of wealth*
*make thy wealth the wealth sevenfold sublime,*[9]
*realize that all earthly wealth is illusory*
*and consider all appearance as the body of truth.*

25

*The beloved son who has been cherished by father and mother,*
*can do them service a hundredfold in their old age;*
*the disciple who has made no solemn vow of retreat*
*can do his teacher service a hundredfold in his old age.*
*But this father like an old dog has been left in the wilderness*
*and his son like a white lion has gone to Ü.*
*The father like an old fox has been left in the wilderness*
*and the son like a young striped tiger has gone to Ü.*
*The father like a barnyard cock has been left in the wilderness*
*and the son like a princely vulture has gone to Ü.*
*The father like an aged bullock with a sagging neck has been*
    *left in the wilderness*
*and the son like a young yak with curved horns has gone to Ü.*
*He whose shape is fairer than a deity has gone to Ü;*
*he whose words are softer than silk has gone to Ü;*
*he whose thoughts are more colourful than embroidery has*
    *gone to Ü;*
*he whose perfume is more delicate than sandalwood has gone*
    *to Ü.*

*26*

In this poem Milarepa rebukes the demons sent to disturb his meditation and invokes the power of his teacher Marpa against them. He urges them to be converted to Marpa and points out to them the superiority of the Greater Vehicle over the Lesser, since the former is responsible for the conception of the Bodhisattva, who, having once attained enlightenment, devotes himself to the service of mankind.

*Behold where the translator Marpa skilled in tongues,*
*the gracious lord without a peer,*
*sits displaying his pure body of bliss*
*upon a triple-stalked lotus throne*
*as a crest-jewel to my mortal's head.*
*He sends forth the light of his grace*
*whiter and purer than the moon in a cloudless sky*
*and opens the fair flower*
*of the lotus of the heart eager for conversion,*
*and makes the anthers of its insight tremble.*
*Do ye see him, ye earth-bound spirits with glancing eyes?*
*If ye see him not it is because of the great darkness in you*
*and your grievous sins*
*from former days in the beginningless round.*
*Unless ye confess them*
*ye are not meet vessels for the doctrine's profundity.*
*Formerly ye were consumed by hatred and wrath,*
*but henceforward ye must mend*
*your evil and deceitful ways,*
*if ye wish to bind yourselves to the faith by a solemn vow.*

*Knowing that its teaching has no other fruit than this:*
*unless ye think clearly upon the cause and effect*
*of every good and evil deed*
*ye will suffer the unbearable miseries of hell.*
*I pray that ye remember to be careful in small things,*
*for though small they may have their consequence.*
*Unless ye have seen objects of the pleasures of sense*
*to be sinful and have banished desire from within you,*
*ye will not be freed from the prison of this world.*
*May ye know in your hearts that all is illusion*
*and rely upon this present help whatever betide, I pray.*
*Unless ye show gratitude in deed*
*to the gracious beings of the six kinds*[1]
*who have engendered you in former lives,*
*ye share the fault of the Lesser Vehicle's error.*
*Therefore may great love*
*teach you enlightenment, I pray.*
*If ye hearken to these goodly teachings and practise them*
*ye will be sages of the Greater Vehicle's path;*
*we shall be brothers in contemplation and exercise,*
*the path we tread in this life will be one and the same;*
*and, where the power of virtue is perfected,*
*in the realms of transcendent purity*
*we shall meet: of that there is no doubt.*

27     Eight sky-travelling goddesses come to Milarepa and beg for spiritual instruction, which he gives them in this song. These are the Buddhist equivalent of fairies and like them defy the ordinary laws of locomotion. They can be gentle or fierce and change their shapes accordingly; when fierce they must be propitiated and made subservient. To achieve this Milarepa commends them to identify themselves with the power of good, as represented by his tutelary deity, who will then direct them in the way of righteousness by his secret influence. If they then meditate upon the knowledge imparted to them as being void, they will eventually attain enlightenment.

*Obeisance to Marpa of Lhobrak.*
*I pray for the gifts of the spirit*
*from the grace of my father and teacher.*

*Ye eight fair daughters of the gods,*
*I have enjoyed meditation after your gift of white rice*
*and the refreshment thereof has increased my devotion.*
*In thanksgiving I preach the doctrine;*
*do ye lend your ears and thereto apply your minds.*
*The kingdom of the gods most pure*
*though it seem real is insubstantial*
*and the tender frolic of young goddess maidens*
*though it be a merry sight soon fades away;*
*the false mirage that deceives the eye*
*though it brings great enjoyment leads to perdition;*
*and the suffering of the sixfold beings of the world*[1]

[44]

*when it is considered greatly moves the heart.*
*Wherefore if ye think to practise the holy doctrine*
*make your supplication to the threefold most precious jewel,*
*the refuge of the faith,*[10]
*and meditate upon the sixfold beings as having formerly*
*engendered you in the round of transmigration.*
*Make oblations to your lord and teacher,*
*give alms to the poor and needy*
*and intend virtue for the benefit of mankind.*
*Meditate continually upon the uncertainty of the hour of death.*
*Believe your own bodies to be the tutelary deity*
*and act according to the words of power of secret utterance;*
*meditate upon your knowledge as the void that passes all*
     *understanding*
*and continually be conscious of the truth.*

# Allegory

## 28

O ye blessed hearers every one,
in the chalice of this body composite
is the body of the innate god.
If ye can raise the lamp of the clear light
truly ye will lighten the body of truth within and without.

In the eyrie of distinctive thought
is the eaglet of enlightenment.
If ye can don the wings of knowledge and art
truly ye will fly in the heaven of omniscience.

In the princely snow mountain of the body
is the lion-cub of discrimination.
If ye can meditate impartially upon the objects of mind and
    sense
truly ye will overcome this world and beyond.

In the ocean of the round of ignorance
is the caravel of the six kinds of being.[1]
If ye can board the ferry-boat of the triple body[5]
truly ye will be saved from the waves of suffering.

In this frame where the baleful imaginings of sense hold sway
is the thief who robs us of salvation.
If ye can catch him with the noose of cunning
truly ye will be delivered from fear.

[46]

*In the body of truth like unto the sky*
*is the jewel fulfilling all desire and need.*
*If ye can meditate undistractedly*
*truly as fruit thereof ye will obtain the triple body.*

*In the keep of this world's castle*
*is shackled all mankind.*
*If ye can free yourselves by the teacher's skill*
*truly ye will no more be prisoners.*

*In the teacher like unto a pearl of great price*
*is a holy spring of counsel.*
*If ye can drink of this with steadfast faith*
*truly ye will quench the sharpness of your thirst.*

## 29

Father, conqueror of the devilish legions,
I make obeisance to thee, Marpa the translator.

Though I myself vaunt not my ancestry,
I am the son of the roaring white lion.
In my mother's womb I perfected the three powers of the mind; [3]
in the years of my childhood I dwelt in the lair;
in the years of my youth I guarded its entrance;
in the years of my manhood I walked the unpeopled snows.
Though the snowstorms whirl I know not fear;
though the precipices yawn I tremble not.

Though I myself vaunt not my ancestry,
I am the son of the eagle, king of birds.
In the egg my wing feathers grew;
in the years of my childhood I dwelt in the eyrie;
in the years of my youth I guarded its entrance;
in the years of my manhood I cleft the vault of heaven.
Though the sky be immense I know not fear;
though the valleys of the earth be narrow I tremble not.

Though I myself vaunt not my ancestry,
I am the son of the great shimmering fish.
In my mother's belly I rolled my golden eye;
in the years of my childhood I dwelt with the fry;
in the years of my youth I led the school;
in the years of my manhood I circled the margins of the lake.

*Though the waves rage fiercely I know not fear;*
*though the nets and the hooks be many I tremble not.*

*Though I myself vaunt not my ancestry,*
*I am the son of the Kargyudpa teacher;*
*in my mother's womb faith arose within me;*
*in the years of my childhood I turned to the doctrine;*
*in the years of my youth I was a disciple;*
*in the years of my manhood I dwelt in the mountains contem-*
*    plative.*
*Though the demons malignantly threaten I know not fear;*
*though the spirits multiply their magical manifestations I*
*    tremble not.*

*The lion rampant in the snow feels not cold in the paws;*
*if the lion in the snow felt cold in his paws*
*there would be little gain in perfecting the three powers.*

*The eagle flying through the heavens cannot fall;*
*if the great eagle flying through the heavens could fall*
*there would be little gain in growing wings.*

*The fish swimming in the water cannot drown;*
*if the fish in the water could drown*
*there would be little gain in being born in the water.*

*The rock of iron is not cleft by stone;*
*if the rock of iron were cleft by stone*
*there would be little gain in melting it down.*

*I, Milarepa, fear not demons;*
*if Milarepa feared demons*
*there would be little gain in knowing reality.*

## 30

*Obeisance to gracious Marpa.*

*Thou who seekest an opportunity to mock me*
*and showest thyself in a horrid ghostly form,*
*thou rock-sprite of the rock of Lingwa,*
*art thou not a demon of evil deeds?*
*I know not how to make my song agreeable*
*but do thou yet hearken to the words of truth.*

*On high in the heaven's azure vault*
*are the sun and moon, auspicious pair.*
*From that palace of the incomparable gods*
*they send forth their rays for the welfare of mankind.*
*When they circle the four continents in their daily task*
*may the demon of eclipse not rise against them as an enemy.*

*Upon the lofty crystal peak of the snow mountain in the east*
*is the auspicious white lion roaring.*
*He is the king of all the subject beasts*
*and as the sign of his greatness eats not the meat of the carcass.*
*When he comes down by the edge of blue slate cliffs*
*may the snowstorm not rise against him as an enemy.*

*Under the leafy canopy of the forest of the south*
*is the auspicious striped tiger.*
*He is the champion of the beasts of prey*
*and as the sign of his glory spares not his own life.*

*When he walks upon the straight path of the abyss*
*may the trap not rise against him as an enemy.*

*In the glittering blue turquoise lake of Mapam in the west*
*is the auspicious white-bellied fish.*
*He is the dancer of the water element*
*and rolls his gold eye marvellously.*
*When he swims after food delectable*
*may the hook not rise against him as an enemy.*

*Upon the fabulous red rock in the north*
*is the auspicious vulture king of birds.*
*He is the seer among winged creatures*
*and in wondrous wise takes no other's life.*
*When he seeks his food upon the triple-peaked mountain*
*may the rope snare not rise against him as an enemy.*

*Upon the rock of Lingwa where the vultures nest*
*is blest Milarepa.*
*He is accomplishing the benefit of his neighbour and himself*
*and as a sign of his truth has given up this world*
*and has quickened his mind to supreme enlightenment.*
*When as his only goal he strives for Buddhahood*
*in this one lifetime and one body,*
*mayest thou, O rock-sprite, not rise against him as an enemy.*

*This song is sixfold of five notable similitudes and their*
*explanation.*
*O rock-sprite, dost thou understand the truth*
*which binds the sayings of these stanzas as a golden chain?*
*In the accumulation of thy deeds thou hast gravely sinned.*
*Let not thy diligence therein increase*
*but hereafter conquer the malice of thine evil mind.*

## ALLEGORY

*If a man knows not all things to be mind*
*the demons of distinctive thought are legion,*
*and if he perceives not mind itself to be void*
*how will he banish these demons false?*
*Thou wicked demoness, harm not, harm not,*
*harm not me who am a man but henceforth depart.*

*31*

I return thanks to my teacher for his favours
and may he of his mercy grant that my soul be ripened into
    deliverance.
To you, blest followers of the faith who are seated here,
I give counsel of profound import in song;
lend me your ears attentively.

The white lion of the snowfields on high
yawns amongst the snow-white peaks
yet fears no other beast,
for the lion's proud habit is to stretch amongst the snows.

The regal vulture of Drakmar
spreads his wings in heaven's expanse
yet fears not lest he fall into the abyss,
for the vulture's proud habit is to cleave the vault of the sky.

In the river and seas beneath
the shimmering fish darts about
yet fears not lest he drown,
for the fish's proud habit is to swim coruscating.

In the branches of the trees that clothe the slopes of Mon
monkeys, long-tailed and short, display their skill
yet fear not lest they fall,
for the monkey's proud habit is to play many a merry game.

ALLEGORY

Under the leafy boughs of the woodland trees
the striped Indian tiger proves his prowess
yet knows not fear,
for the tiger's nature is to glory in his cunning.

In the forests of Singghala
Milarepa meditates upon the Void
yet fears not lest his meditation fail,
for his proud habit is to concentrate prolongedly.

In the pure cycle of the sphere of truth
he enjoys undistracted experience
yet fears not error in its significance,
for his proud habit is to establish himself in reality.

In the experience of the life-force travelling its inward course
he is troubled by delusive visions sent to hinder him
yet deviates not from the true interpretation thereof,
for his is the boast that these signs of progress arise.

From the inherent energy of his successful concentration
crowd in upon him a multitude of lofty and mean thoughts
yet he holds his mind in abeyance from them,
for his is the stage at which myriad ideas are bound to appear.

By the ripened power of the law of cause and fruit
he beholds the very shape of virtue and of vice
yet is not disturbed in his rapture,
for his is the word of infallible truth that divides them asunder.

*32*

*My steed has the fleetness of the discriminating mind.*
*He glories proudly in the silk tassels of equanimity;*
*he has the sheepskin of success amidst life's illusion*
*and the gaudy saddle of bright self-knowledge is set thereon,*
*held tight by the girths of this world's triple pain.[11]*
*He bears the crupper of knowledge and art, its complement;*
*he has the bridle of retention of the breath upon his head*
*and about his eyebrows the waving fringe of concentration*
*upon the tip of his nose at dawn, midday and dusk,*
*and upon his forehead the embossed crest-piece of the flood of*
     *inward peace.*
*His mouth is guided by the reins of the magic body;*
*he is struck by the whip of the flowing river of the mind.*
*He is proved first in the race on the plain of transcendent*
     *experience.*
*Such is my sage's stallion.*
*If it flees, it is freed from the mire of this world.*
*If it pursues, it reaches the haven of perfect purity.*

33

A traveller comes upon Milarepa by the wayside and begs counsel. He is wearing his usual Tibetan riding-boots of deerskin with thick felt soles, decorated with a gay design in silk and embellished with brass studs. Milarepa uses them as a symbol of the world and its cramping effect upon the sage.

Behold, this patrimony of the three kingdoms of this world
is shrouded in the gloomy darkness of ignorance.
The meads of covetousness are a deep slough of mire.
The fens of envy are full of prickly thorns.
The wild dog of anger barks and snaps.
The crag of pride towers on the mountain peak.
When I have forded the river of life
I pray that I may flee to the plain of great bliss.
In my boots the spotted deerskin of the perishable stuff of
        illusion
and the double felt soles of the perverse will of this world
are sewn together with faith in action's cause and fruit.
The boots are green-embroidered with manifold sensual delights
and the silk of their embroidery is the mind free from all desire.
They have embossed brass studs of the pursuit of attainment
and are fastened by the buckles of the three original bonds:[12]
these are my sage's Chinese boots.

*34*

O almsgiver puffed up with pride,
Ngendzong the rich, hearken to me.
Throughout the three months of springtime
when every Tibetan ploughs his own field
I too, the sage, plough a field.
Upon the hard ground of primordial suffering
I have put the manure of faith, the harbinger,
and have watered it copiously with the fivefold nectar.[13]
A husbandman full of confidence,
I have sowed the seed of freedom from the error of reflective
    thought.
Having yoked the oxen of transcendence of duality
I attached the ploughshare of wisdom,
and guided by the sacred scriptures
drove the plough of imperturbability,
using the whip of instant zeal.
The seed is hardy and strong;
the shoot of holiness will spring up;
the ear will ripen in due time.
Thou dost the husbandry of this world;
I do the husbandry of eternal growth.
At the time of harvest we shall surely see increase;
and when it is past we shall surely vie in merriment.

*This is sung as a parable;*
*this is my song of husbandry.*
*Make thy heart virtuous who art puffed up with pride;*
*act to thine own benefit and accumulate meritorious deeds.*

*35*

O almsgiver, who dost ply me with question after question,
thou who hast the power of benevolence, hearken to me.
Knowest thou or knowest thou not my name?
If thou knowest it not,
I am Milarepa.
I am one who is a penitent;
I am one who has meditated mightily with zeal;
I am a sage who has forsaken partiality.
This staff that I hold in my hand,
which grew first on the side of an Indian crag,
later bowed and succumbed to an Indian knife
and finally was bound with a soft leather thong.
Its origin was in Mon in the south;
its lading was upon the yak of the Great Vehicle;
its journeying was through the market-places;
its offering was to one of the faithful.
Such is this staff of mine.
Understandest thou the meaning of this or not?
If thou understandest not the meaning of this
hearken while I explain it to thee clearly.
The cutting off of the bamboo at the root
signifies the cutting off of the root cause of this world.
The cutting off of the bamboo at the top
signifies the cutting off of error caused by doubt.
The falling short of two cubits' standard

signifies the rejection of the double standard of the common
    man.

The natural goodness and suppleness of the bamboo
signify the everlasting goodness of the primordial mind.

The sweetness of the sap and beauty of the colour of the bamboo
signify the cultivation of the truth of the essential mind.

The pliability of the upright bamboo
signifies the practice of the unerring truth.

The grooved stem of the bamboo
signifies the perfection of the way that leads to the flow of
    holiness.

The four sections of the bamboo
signify fulfilment of the four immeasurable virtues.[14]

The three joints of the bamboo
signify the perfection of the threefold body[5] in its incorrupt-
    ability.

The unchanging colour of the bamboo
signifies the unchangeability of the fundamental truth.

The roundness of the sections of the bamboo
signifies the inactivity of the very truth.

The ever white lustre of the bamboo
signifies the spotlessness of the body of truth.

The hollowness of the bamboo
signifies the void of all things real.

The speckles upon the bamboo
signify knowledge of the truth as a single seed-essence.

The black flecks of the bamboo
signify that the cotton-clad sage of Tibet
possesses subtle discernment.

The ever noble ancestry of the bamboo
signifies his dutiful practice of the doctrine.

*The pleasant comeliness of the bamboo*
*signifies his zeal for the faith of mankind.*
*The iron tip with which the bamboo is shod*
*signifies the sage's wandering in the mountains.*
*The copper sheath of the handle*
*signifies his power over the sky-travelling goddesses.*
*The iron nails upon the bamboo*
*signify the sage's great perseverance.*
*The ring of brass set thereon*
*signifies his abundant inner excellence.*
*The leather strap attached to it*
*signifies the pliant wisdom of the sage.*
*The double lacing of the cord*
*signifies his progress on the path of union of the two in one.*
*The intertwining of the original cord with another like unto it*
*signifies his union with the original triple body.*
*The bone almsdish attached thereto*
*signifies the sage's roaming throughout the world.*
*The tinder-pouch attached thereto*
*signifies his friendship towards all creatures.*
*The white conch-shell attached thereto*
*signifies his tracing of the sacred diagram of the truth.*
*The small piece of tigerskin attached thereto*
*signifies his utter fearlessness.*
*The mirror attached thereto*
*signifies the dawning within him of perfect intuition.*
*The sharp knife attached thereto*
*signifies his cutting off of the torments of affliction.*
*The single crystal ball attached thereto*
*signifies the renunciation of desire's impurity.*
*The rosary tied of ivory beads attached thereto*

signifies the tie of love for his teacher.
The set of bells attached thereto
signifies his preaching of the gospel throughout all lands.
The woollen and cotton cloth, the white and red, attached thereto
signifies the multitude of his disciples.
The use thereof by the sage's hand
signifies his conversion of laymen by the right method.
The enquiry after its meaning
signifies the inclination to reverence.
The meeting with me
signifies the making of a former prayer.
This song of the meaning of this white staff
all gods and men can understand.
Since thy devout belief makes thee possessed of its religious
    significance,
Do thou ever practise the holy faith in happiness.

Milarepa here in allegory exposes the dangers that
the disciple is likely to meet in his subtle contem-
plation and describes the way for him to preserve
himself unharmed from such ghostly assaults. He          *36*
must persevere and stand firm, using the power of
the magical spells that he has been taught, to bind
his demon adversaries to servitude and then to
reabsorb them so that his mind is stilled and made
fit for the beatific vision.

*In the east in the glorious empire of China*
*a Chinese woman weaves a silken web.*
*If the shuttle of her inner thread go not awry*
*she will not be dismayed by the swift wind of outer time,*
*but performing her task with inward care*
*will complete her silken cloth.*

*In the north in the kingdom of lower Hor*
*a mighty champion goes forth to battle.*
*If he raise not to rebellion the ghostly world within*
*he will not fear the host of Gesar without,*
*but protecting himself by exorcism*
*will be victorious.*

*In the west in the precipitous country of Persia*
*is the brazen gate of the citadel of the warrior horde.*
*If its sea of molten brass within be not stirred amiss*
*it will not yield to the slings and arrows without,*
*but being free from inner flaw*
*will resist their blows.*

*In the south in the thunder-bolt land of Nepal*
*stands the healing sandalwood tree.*
*If the ghostly axe is not laid to it within*
*it will not be cleft by the axe of the dweller in Mon without,*
*but, withstanding all inner destruction,*
*will grow on in the forest.*

*In the solitary place of Chubar of Drin*
*art thou, Milarepa, the goodly meditator.*
*If thou make not thine inward discernment a demon adversary*
*thou wilt not fear the devilish assaults without,*
*but, purifying thy native mind within,*
*will become a sage.*

*Thou hast trained thyself to control thy sensual imaginings*
*and upon the craggy mountain of the void of truth*
*hast sought out the castle of immovable contemplation;*
*hast girded on the armour of mental enlightenment*
*and sharpened the weapons of wisdom and mercy.*
*Though the devilish legions compass thee round about*
*thou wilt not flee to the city of inclination.*
*Though the world of death's king rise up as thine enemy*
*thou wilt not be vanquished by his army but will surely win the*
  *victory.*
*Yet the appearance of outward things desirable is wondrous to*
  *behold*
*and the concentration of inward quiet induces lassitude;*
*the desire for sense-delights is a long-lived companion,*
*and when thou art immersed in the stream of vision that*
  *passes understanding*
*the demon of discernment is clever at finding means of enmity.*

Lying ever in wait upon the strait way between the abyss of
     hope and fear
he may catch thee in the noose of selfishness.
But thou dost watch over thy memory and consciousness
and, being one who dost guard well thy castle, art a sage.

This song has four similitudes which with the explanation
     thereof make five.
Its words of good tiding are pearls strung on a necklace
and its explanation is a mirror beauteous to the soul.
Learn to understand it, O disciple fortunate.

# The Function of Number

The six following poems have been chosen to show the importance of number in Milarepa's teaching. The Indian mind is given to analysis and classi-

37  fication, which makes the Buddhist Canon often so tedious to the Western reader; we have many examples of this in our text: the twofold merit, the three bonds, the eight worldly principles and the like. But with Milarepa number gains a metaphysical significance as it did for Aristotle: each of the integers is assigned its own function in the scheme of the universe, the role of the number three being of particular importance. As in the Christian revelation Milarepa teaches a unity which is also a trinity.

*The teachers, Tilopa, Naropa and Marpa are three:*
*these three are the teachers of Mila.*
*If thou dost desire these three teachers,*
*follow him who is the cotton-clad.*

*Teacher, tutelary god and sky-travelling goddess are three:*
*these three are the worshipping places of Mila.*
*If thou dost desire these three worshipping places,*
*follow him who is the cotton-clad.*

*Buddha, doctrine and congregation are three;*
*these three are Mila's places of refuge.*

*If thou dost desire these three places of refuge,*
*follow him who is the cotton-clad.*

*Contemplation, meditation and consummation are three:*
*these three are Mila's exercises.*
*If thou dost desire these three exercises,*
*follow him who is the cotton-clad.*

*Ore mountain, snow mountain and slate mountain are three:*
*these three are Mila's places of attainment.*
*If thou wouldest these places of attainment,*
*follow him who is the cotton-clad.*

*Stag, antelope and mountain sheep are three:*
*these three are the cattle in Mila's byre.*
*If thou wouldest these three kinds of cattle,*
*follow him who is the cotton-clad.*

*Lynx, leopard and wolf are three:*
*these three are the dogs at Mila's door.*
*If thou wouldest these three kinds of dogs,*
*follow him who is the cotton-clad.*

*Blackbird, ptarmigan and hawk are three:*
*these three are the fowls in Mila's yard.*
*If thou wouldest these three kinds of fowls,*
*follow him who is the cotton-clad.*

*Sun, moon and stars are three:*
*these three are the lights of Mila's eye.*
*If thou wouldest these three lights of the eye,*
*follow him who is the cotton-clad.*

*God, demon and hermit are three:*
*these three are Mila's neighbours.*
*If thou wouldest these three neighbours,*
*follow him who is the cotton-clad.*

*Monkey, marmot and bear are three:*
*these three are Mila's playmates.*
*If thou wouldest these three playmates,*
*follow him who is the cotton-clad.*

*Bliss and beatific vision and transcendence of thought are three:*
*these three are Mila's comforters.*
*If thou wouldest these three comforters,*
*follow him who is the cotton-clad.*

*Nettle, radish and dandelion are three:*
*these three are Mila's foods.*
*If thou wouldest these three foods,*
*follow him who is the cotton-clad.*

*Rock water, glacier water and clay water are three:*
*these three are Mila's drinks.*
*If thou wouldest these three drinks,*
*follow him who is the cotton-clad.*

*Breath, nervous energy and life-force are three:*
*these three are Mila's garments.*
*If thou wouldest have these three garments,*
*follow him who is the cotton-clad.*

*38*

*I praise and worship with body, speech and mind at the feet*
*of Marpa the great translator and interpreter,*
*the abode of fulfilment of every need and wish,*
*the glorious mountain of virtues sublime.*

*Leadership, meditation and counsel, these three*
*cause the rise of the pain of partiality.*
*If thou desirest to be established in impartiality*
*knowest thou how to be an idle simpleton?*

*Patrimony, wealth and generosity, these three*
*cause the bondage of the three worlds' round.*[15]
*If thou desirest to be freed from the river of suffering*
*knowest thou how to cease all strong affection?*

*Self-desire, self-deceit and fraud, these three*
*cause the fall into the three hells.*
*If thou desirest to gain the path of heaven's freedom*
*knowest thou how to keep thy mind upright?*

*Teaching, friendship and discussion, these three*
*cause the rise of pride and jealousy.*
*If thou desirest to take to heart the holy truth*
*knowest thou how to choose a lowly station?*

*Home, position and regard for opinion, these three*
*cause the undoing of the sage's meditation.*
*If thou desirest to preserve thine innate wisdom*
*knowest thou how to be unashamedly humble?*

*Lordship, servants and disciples, these three*
*cause the chastisement of distraction.*
*If thou desirest to learn solitude*
*knowest thou how to be lordless and servantless?*

*Sorcery, witchcraft and malediction, these three*
*cause the risk of the sage's life.*
*If thou desirest to pursue the holy truth to the uttermost*
*knowest thou how to be as unassuming as a wren?*

*This song of the seven several remedies*
*for the seven causes of transgression against the holy truth*
*must dawn upon thy heart and be received therein.*
*See that thou attain illumination through virtue.*

## 39

O lord, who hidest thy divinity in human form,
translator of terms hard to express,
obeisance to thee, O merciful father Marpa.

Though I am no singer to kindle the feelings,
since thou sayest, sing a song, sing a song,
therefore I sing a song of the nature of things.

Thunder, lightning and southern cloud are three
and when they come they come from the sky itself
and when they vanish they vanish into the sky itself.

Rainbow, fog and mist are three
and when they come they come from the air itself
and when they vanish they vanish into the air itself.

Sap, harvest and fruit are three
and when they come they come from the earth itself
and when they vanish they vanish into the earth itself.

Forest, flower and leaf are three
and when they come they come from the mountain itself
and when they vanish they vanish into the mountain itself.

River, foam and wave are three
and when they come they come from the sea itself
and when they vanish they vanish into the sea itself.

*Inclination, desire and grasping are three*
*and when they come they come from self-consciousness itself*
*and when they vanish they vanish into self-consciousness itself.*

*Self-knowledge, self-enlightenment and self-deliverance are three*
*and when they come they come from mind itself*
*and when they vanish they vanish into mind itself.*

*Uncreate, unobstructed and ineffable are three*
*and when they come they come from reality itself*
*and when they vanish they vanish into reality itself.*

*Appearance, percept and concept of a demon are three*
*and when they come they come from the sage himself*
*and when they vanish they vanish into the sage himself.*

*Now as devils are the magic show of the mind*
*the sage is deluded if he considers demons to have reality,*
*not knowing his own visions to be void.*
*For the root of delusion comes from the mind*
*and he who knows the inwardness of mind*
*sees that the clear light within neither comes nor goes.*
*And when the mind that is deceived by the appearance of*
       *outward things*
*has discerned the nature of appearance,*
*it knows that there is no distinction between appearance and the*
       *void.*
*Again when the mind discerns the nature of meditation*
*it also discerns what is not meditation,*
*and that there is no distinction between the two.*
*For distinctive thought is the root of delusion*
*and such thought has never been of the ultimate truth.*

*But he who takes the nature of the sky*
*as a likeness of the nature of the mind and all its works*
*conceives reality aright.*
*So do thou as contemplation contemplate the truth that passeth*
    *understanding*
*and as meditation enter the sphere of imperturbability*
*and as consummation cleave to unobstructed spontaneity*
*and as fruit eschew the distinctions of hope and fear.*
*Thus do thou fulfil thy religious destiny.*

## 40

To cleave to a wise teacher
is called the guide to this world and beyond.

To give charity unstintingly
is to lay up provender for the journey.

To behold the moon rise in the darkness of percipience
is to lay up a guide.

To devote to the faith all things acquired
is to lay up a ferry-boat.

If your contemplation is free from partiality
your meditation will be free from distraction;
and if your consummation accords with the faith
your holy vow will be pleasing to your teacher,
and your fruit will be to have no regret in the hour of death.

Counsellor, almsgiver and disciple are three
and I the sage have little need of them
but ye of the world have need of them.

Obeisance, politeness and flattery are three
and I the sage have little need of them
but the worldling has need of them.

Goods, chattels and entertainment are three
and I the sage have little need of them
but the seeker after celebrity has need of them.

*Bathing, purification and scrupulousness are three*
*and I the sage have little need of them*
*but young men have need of them.*

*These are twelve needless things*
*and I have time for none of them:*
*such is my cotton-clad sage's boast*
*and do ye who are assembled mark it well within your hearts.*
*If ye wish for happiness practise the holy faith;*
*if ye weary of bustle cleave to the lonely place;*
*if ye have great zeal abide in solitude;*
*if ye desire enlightenment be hardy in meditation*
*and ye shall surely conquer your devilish foes.*

## 41

*Obeisance to the lords the teachers.*

*Buddha, doctrine and congregation are three.*
*These three are the external refuge.*
*I, the mortal, delight in taking refuge in them:*
*It is good that ye too should take refuge in them.*

*Teacher, tutelary god and sky-travelling goddess are three.*
*These three are the eternal refuge.*
*I delight in taking refuge in them:*
*It is good that ye too should take refuge in them.*

*Breath, nervous energy and life-force are three*
*these three are the secret refuge.*
*I delight in taking refuge in them:*
*it is good that ye too should take refuge in them.*

*Appearance, Void and distinctionless are three.*
*These three are the refuge of truth.*
*I delight in taking refuge in them:*
*it is good that ye too should take refuge in them.*

*From the weariness of incessant suffering,*
*upon the rotting habitation of the illusory body*
*the shower of the days and hours falls*
*and the rain-drops of the years and months beat down.*
*Verily the rotting habitation of the illusory body perishes.*

*It is meet to prepare for the rain by a willingness to die.*
*Thus like the lengthening shadows of the dying day*
*though a man flee farther and farther*
*yet they follow him closer and closer.*
*Verily he who flees sees not liberation.*

*The sight of a believer dying*
*preaches encouragement towards virtue:*
*he beholds joy in everything.*
*The sight of a sinner dying*
*preaches the difference between virtue and vice:*
*he beholds repentance in everything.*
*The sight of a rich man dying*
*preaches that wealth is an enemy:*
*he beholds the power to give in everything.*
*The sight of an old man dying*
*preaches the impermanence of life:*
*he beholds sorrow in everything.*
*The sight of a young man dying*
*preaches that life admits not of leisure:*
*he beholds earnest endeavour in everything.*

*Happiness is the due of father and mother*
*but how can this be if their children afflict them?*
*There is warmth beneath a soft fur*
*but how can this be for him who has not worn one?*
*The fruit of husbandry does away with poverty*
*but how can this be for him who cannot work?*
*A horse has the swiftness of the wind*
*but how can this be for him who cannot ride?*
*Practice of the faith brings happiness to life*
*but how can this be for him who cannot practise it?*

*Wherefore deprive thyself of food and give alms*
*and deprive thyself of sleep and practise virtue.*
*Be mindful of the suffering of hell;*
*think thereon and practise the holy faith.*

*42*

*Ye faithful disciples who have travelled hither,*
*do ye earnestly practise the holy doctrine or not?*
*Has faith been born in the depths of your being or not?*
*If ye intend to practise the holy doctrine with all your heart*
*and are not unstable in your faith,*
*take as an example this altogether delusive world.*
*Ask your mind its meaning.*
*Have ye looked upon outward appearance as an example or*
 *have ye not?*
*When ye look upon appearance as an example*
*the first example is the hail upon the plain;*
*the second is the turquoise flower;*
*the third is the mountain spate;*
*the fourth is the waving corn harvest;*
*the fifth is the profusion of rich silks;*
*the sixth is the precious jewel;*
*the seventh is the moon in its three phases;*
*the eighth is the darling son.*
*Thus far now ye have not repeated these words*
*but unless ye repeat the rest of this song*
*the words will not reveal their true significance.*

*If ye would know the meaning of these words:*
*the hail upon the plain vanishes up to the heavens;*
*this gives an example of change;*

*this is after the manner of transitoriness.*
*Ponder upon this truth and practise the holy doctrine.*

*The turquoise flower is killed by frost;*
*this gives an example of change;*
*this is after the manner of transitoriness.*
*Ponder upon this truth and practise the holy doctrine.*

*The mountain-spate is swallowed up by the valley below;*
*this gives an example of change;*
*this is after the manner of transitoriness.*
*Ponder upon this truth and practise the holy doctrine.*

*The waving corn harvest is reaped;*
*this gives an example of change;*
*this is after the manner of transitoriness.*
*Ponder upon this truth and practise the holy doctrine.*

*The profusion of rich silks is pierced by the awl;*
*this gives an example of change;*
*this is after the manner of transitoriness.*
*Ponder upon this truth and practise the holy doctrine.*

*The precious jewel, having been found, is lost;*
*this gives an example of change;*
*this is after the manner of transitoriness.*
*Ponder upon this truth and practise the holy doctrine.*

*The moon in its three phases, having risen, sets;*
*this gives an example of change;*
*this is after the manner of transitoriness.*
*Ponder upon this truth and practise the holy doctrine.*

*The darling son, having been born, dies;*
*this gives an example of change;*
*this is after the manner of transitoriness.*
*Ponder upon this truth and practise the holy doctrine.*

*These eight wonderful examples*
*I expound to you who have accompanied me, in return for your*
      *reverence.*
*There is no end to the deeds that may be done.*
*In whatsoever pleases you, practise the holy doctrine.*
*While ye think that ye have leisure your life is spent.*
*Since ye know not when comes the hour of death*
*ponder upon this truth and practise the holy doctrine.*

# The Seed of Enlightenment

## 43

This is the solitary place of Changchub-dzong.*
Above, the white snow peak of the puissant demon towers;
below, the faithful almsgivers dwell;
behind, the mountain is veiled with a curtain of white silk;
before, the forest groves that satisfy the heart abound
and the grassy meads and spacious pastures spread.
About the lovely fragrant lotuses
the dragon-flies hum busily.
Upon the banks of the ponds and pools
the water-fowl turn back their necks and stare.
In the boughs of the spreading trees
the hosts of pretty birds descant sweet harmonies.
In the scent-laden breeze
the branches of the trees perform a dance.
In the tops of the tall trees conspicuous
the monkeys long-tailed and short perform their feats of skill.
In the broad green meadows lush
the four-footed beasts are scattered browsing.
The herders who watch over them
agreeably tune their voices and their pipes.
The slaves to worldly covetousness
ply their trade and spread their wares upon the ground.
Beholding this, I the sage
upon my precious rock that is visible afar

* i.e. the stronghold of enlightenment.

consider appearance the similitude of impermanence,
and meditate upon the pleasures of sense as the reflection in
      water.
I look upon this life as the illusion of a dream,
meditate with compassion for the ignorant
and feed upon the void of space.
I meditate in undisturbed ecstasy
and all the manifold images that arise before the mind,
aye all the things that the three worlds[15] contain,
appear insubstantial most miraculously.

## 44

*To the lord Marpa my teacher do I address my prayer.*

*Knowest thou or knowest thou not the virtues of this place?*
*If thou knowest not the virtues thereof,*
*this hermitage is the sky stronghold of the recluse's blessing.*
*Above, the purple southern clouds gather;*
*below, the blue waters of the Tsangpo roll;*
*behind, the red rock to heaven towers;*
*before, the meadows with flowers are pied;*
*beasts of prey roar upon the verge;*
*the regal vulture wheels apart;*
*fine rain falls from out the sky;*
*bees sing their song without surcease;*
*deer and wild asses in frolic skip, the mother with her young;*
*monkeys long-tailed and short display their skill;*
*larks quire many-tongued, the mother with her chicks;*
*the divine bird, the ptarmigan, calls out his cry;*
*the brook murmurs pleasantly over the stones.*
*These passing voices in their variety*
*are the companions of the soul.*
*The virtues of this place are inconceivable.*
*I have expressed my joyous heart in song;*
*I have uttered counsel with my lips.*
*Ye almsgivers, men and women gathered here,*
*follow me and do as I do;*
*renounce evil deeds and ensue the good.*

45

*O fortunate and holy mortals,*
*Know ye not that this life is deceit?*
*Know ye not that enjoyment is illusion?*
*Know ye not that the world is a passing show?*
*Know ye not that happiness is a dream?*
*Know ye not that praise and blame are insubstantial?*
*Know ye not that appearance is the mind itself?*
*Know ye not that the mind itself is Buddhahood?*
*Know ye not that Buddhahood is the body of truth?*
*Know ye not that the body of truth is truth itself?*
*When ye reflect, all appearances are compacted out of mind.*
*Contemplate the mind by day and night.*
*From contemplation of the mind comes beatific vision;*
*abide in that beatitude.*
*Naught is more apt than the great symbol of the void*
*for consideration of reality;*
*abide in the state that passes understanding.*
*When ye attain profitable equanimity untroubled by the*
    *affections*
*the course of your meditations will be free from self;*
*whatever happens will be in essence vacuous;*
*your consciousness will be free from thought and thoughtlessness;*
*ye will enjoy the taste of the uncreate.*
*If ye would have knowledge of such meditation*
*ye must meditate upon this effective symbol*
*and upon life's concentrated force.*

*Ye must meditate upon the deity, repeating the words of power,*
*and upon the source of purity and such exalted things.*
*These are the means of entering the path of the Great Vehicle.*
*When ye meditate upon these things assiduously,*
*though ye do not succeed in rooting out desire and hatred,*
*know that whatever appears is your own mind-stuff*
*and that the mind itself is void.*
*If ye dwell in wisdom inseparably*
*all the observances of the law, oblations and the like,*
*are thus perfectly fulfilled.*

46

*O hearer Pedarbum,*
*hearken, noble maiden full of faith.*

*If there is joy in meditation upon the sky,*
*the southern cloud is the magic creation of the sky;*
*make thyself like unto the sky itself.*

*If there is joy in meditation upon the sun and moon,*
*the planets and fixed stars are the magic creation of the sun and*
    *moon;*
*make thyself like unto the sun and moon themselves.*

*If there is joy in meditation upon the mountain,*
*the fruit-trees are the magic creation of the mountain;*
*make thyself like the mountain itself.*

*If there is joy in meditation upon the sea,*
*the waves are the magic creation of the sea;*
*make thyself like unto the sea itself.*

*If there is joy in meditation upon thine own mind,*
*distinctive thought is the magic creation of the mind;*
*make thyself like unto the mind itself.*

## 47

To the holy teacher, thy support,
again and again offer thy prayer with all thy heart.
When thou meditatest upon the tutelary god and the sky-
    travelling goddess,
again and again practise the exercise of creation in all its
    clarity.
When thou meditatest upon impermanence and death,
again and again think of the uncertainty of the hour of death.
When thou meditatest upon the great symbol of the void,
again and again meditate upon that which is infinitely small.
When thou meditatest upon sentient beings as having engendered
    thee in thy previous lives,
again and again give grateful thanks to them.
When thou meditatest upon the profound ear-whispered
    teachings,
put forth zeal and energy.
When thou pursuest the holy truth to the uttermost,
without exaltation or abasement preserve the proper mean.
When thou contemplatest in accordance with the faith,
contemplate one thing only and flit not hither and thither.
When thou cultivatest the holy faith,
renounce all worldly activity.
When the gods provide sustenance,
there is no need for toil and trouble.
That covetous hoarding brings not increase

*is the acknowledged truth of the sky-travelling goddesses.*
*Therefore cast away all thought for the future;*
*therefore renounce this life in thy heart.*

## 48

The excellent teacher of great compassion;
the precious trinity of goodly refuge; [10]
the sky-travelling goddesses, defenders of the faith mighty
    in power:
to these aforesaid I bow.

Since I know not how to compose sweet songs
the blessing of the mystic father be upon these my words.
In their truth the thought of the Buddha is expressed.
O faithful meditatress Salleo,
in the polished mirror of my mind
behold the expanse of the immaculate heavens.

Go to meditate in the mountains, the solitary place
hallowed by former sages,
and while the spirit drives thee to dwell there
contemplate the nature of the mind our governor.
I will expound this manner of contemplation,
wherefore hearken with undistracted mind, O Salleo.

When thou first dwellest at the door of the doctrine,
unvarying faith is a great boon;
take yonder mountain on high as an example
and make a meditation upon that which is immovable.

To arouse the virtue of Buddhahood
I pray thee to resign the vehicle of happiness and suffering;

*take yonder river beneath as an example*
*and make a meditation upon that which flows unceasingly.*

*To ensue the blessing of the teacher*
*I pray that thy veneration may never have surcease;*
*take this sky as an example*
*and make a meditation upon that which has neither centre nor*
    *circumference.*

*To contemplate the truth of reality*
*I pray thee to unite art and wisdom;*
*take the twain, the sun and moon, as an example*
*and make a meditation upon the shadowless clarity.*

*To realize that all sentient creatures have engendered thee in*
    *thy previous lives*
*I pray thee to comprise them all in thy compassion;*
*take the ocean beneath as an example*
*and make a meditation upon that which is undisturbed.*

*To behold thine own mind manifestly*
*I pray thee to make conjuration according to the teacher's*
    *commandment.*
*Take this solid earth as an example*
*and make a meditation upon that which is unchangeable.*

*To become a fit vessel for my counsels*
*I pray thee to have an abiding faith in the primordial spirit.*
*Contemplate closely this mind of thine*
*and make a meditation upon that which is undesignated.*

*To cause the world of appearance to open as a book*
*I pray thee to study thine own mind;*
*lay up the provision of unceasing almsgiving*
*at all times and in every manner.*

*Deck thyself in the beautiful jewel of morality;*
*put on the blessed habit of patience;*
*mount upon the magic horse of zeal,*
*hasten to the city of sublime ecstasy;*
*become rich in the wealth of wisdom.*
*Forget not the gratitude due to thy teacher,*
*offer him the hundredfold sacrifice of mind and understanding.*
*Then thou mayest have access to the truth,*
    *O maiden full of faith.*

*49*

For true contemplation contemplate thine own mind:
if thou seek contemplation elsewhere than in the mind
thou art indeed like a man seeking a jewel of clay,
  O teacher Lharje.

For true meditation let not the fruit of distraction arise:
if the fruit of distraction arise therein
thou art indeed like a man using a torch by day,
  O teacher Lharje.

For true consummation accept not nor reject thy visions:
if thou continue acceptance and rejection
Thou art indeed like a bee caught in a net,
  O teacher Lharje.

For a true surety rest in the certitude of the beatific vision:
if thou seek elsewhere a surety, which will prove insecure,
thou art indeed like a man turning a spring uphill,
  O teacher Lharje.

For true fruit foster true knowledge in thy mind:
if thou seek elsewhere fruit, which cannot be found,
thou art indeed like a frog jumping into the air,
  O teacher Lharje.

For the true teacher enquire of thine own mind:
if thou seek a teacher elsewhere than in thy mind

*thou art indeed like a man who has lost his mind,*
* O teacher Lharje.*

*Verily all appearances are creations of thine own mind,*
* O teacher Lharje.*

# Old Age and Death

50

O hearer Pedarbum,
hearken, revered maiden full of faith.
The journey of the hereafter is longer than the journey of this life.
Hast thou made ready provision therefor?
If thou hast not made ready provision therefor
pray that thou mayest have the spirit of giving and give.
He who dwells pent up with the enemy called avarice,
though he thinks himself profited, works harm alone.
Knowest thou avarice to be an enemy?
If thou knowest, see that thou cast it behind thee.

O hearer Pedarbum,
the darkness of the hereafter is blacker than the darkness of this
     life.
Hast thou made ready a lamp therefor?
If thou hast not made ready a lamp therefor
pray that thou mayest have the clear light and meditate.
He who sleeps senseless in the arms of the foe called darkness,
though he thinks himself profited, works harm alone.
Knowest thou darkness to be an enemy?
If thou knowest, see that thou cast it behind thee.

O hearer Pedarbum,
the fear of the hereafter is greater than the fear of this life.
Hast thou made ready a guide therefor?
If thou hast not made ready a guide therefor

*pray that thou mayest receive the holy truth and practise it.*
*He who lets himself be hindered by the enemy called kinsfolk,*
*though he thinks himself profited, works harm alone.*
*Knowest thou kinsfolk to be an enemy?*
*If thou knowest, see that thou cast them behind thee.*

*O hearer Pedarbum,*
*the path of the hereafter is longer than the path of this life.*
*Hast thou made ready a horse therefor?*
*If thou hast not made ready a horse therefor*
*pray that thou mayest have zeal and be diligent.*
*He who is led deceitfully by the enemy called sloth,*
*though he thinks himself profited, works his own harm alone.*
*Knowest thou sloth to be an enemy?*
*If thou knowest, see that thou cast it behind thee.*

*51*

Ye who delight thus in castles and cottages,
remember that when ye die ye leave an empty habitation.
Ye who delight thus in heaping words of abuse,
remember that when ye die ye go to a place where ye have
     neither protection nor refuge.
Ye who delight thus in a multitude of kinsfolk and friends,
remember that when ye die ye will be parted from all your
     acquaintances.
Ye who delight thus in your retinue of servants, your sons and
     your wealth,
remember that when ye die ye will go without riches with empty
     hands and naked.
Ye who delight thus in your strength and beauty and skill,
remember that when ye die ye must contemplate the threefold
     body.[5]
Ye who delight thus in your quick mind and healthy constitution,
remember that when ye die your knowledge is of no avail.
Ye who delight thus in sweetmeats,
remember that when ye die ye will crave naught but water.
Therefore remember all these things and practise the holy faith.

## 52

Now, almsgiver who payest goodly heed,
to explain the suffering of old age:
when the constituents of the body grow frail
the suffering of old age is a desolation.
The frame which was born erect is bowed;
the step which was firmly set is staggering;
The locks which were born black are white;
the eye, the most limpid of the senses, grows dim;
the head, the chief of the limbs, shakes;
the ear, which hears sounds, is deaf;
the sea of blood in the cheeks dries up;
the nose, the foundation of good looks, is bent;
the shell-like teeth, the most excellent of the bones, fall out;
the tongue, the king of speech, stammers;
lice multiply like hidden debts.
Though the aged man invite friends to a banquet, they run
    away from him;
though he avoids despondency over suffering it returns again;
though he speaks truth there is no listener.
His children whom he brought up lovingly grow angry at him;
no one shows gratitude at the splendour of his possessions.
He is slow to die, they say and heap curses on him.
Moreover unless a man comprehend a truth that transcends old
    age
the suffering of old age surpasses his imagining.

*Not to remember the holy faith in old age
is the retribution of former deeds.
Now while a man still has breath
it is good to practise the holy faith.*

## 53

*Alas, ye sentient beings of the world!*
*Though ye guard and guard your body like green turquoises*
*circumstance will make them fall like aged trees.*
*Give undistracted heed upon occasion due.*

*Though ye accumulate and accumulate wealth like honey*
*circumstance will dissipate it like hoar-frost.*
*Give undistracted heed upon occasion due.*

*Though ye associate and associate with friends like wild deer*
*circumstance will come upon them like a hunter.*
*Give undistracted heed upon occasion due.*

*Though ye cherish and cherish your children like eggs*
*circumstance will strike them like a stone upon a path.*
*Give undistracted heed upon occasion due.*

*Though your beauty be fair as a flower in the wilderness*
*circumstance will beset it like hail.*
*Awaken instant revulsion from the world upon occasion due.*

*Though ye be good, good friends like mother and son*
*circumstance will make you quarrel like hostile relations.*
*Waken compassion for sentient beings upon occasion due.*

*Though ye bask in happiness like the sun*
*misfortune will overwhelm you like a whirlwind.*
*Give charity to the needy upon occasion due.*

*Moreover, ye almsgiving men and women assembled here,*
*if ye cannot practise a single part of the sacred and divine faith*
*your long span of life will be a long sinning*
*and your exertion in manifold works will be a work of affliction.*

## 54

I bow at the feet of the teacher, the Buddha of the three times.
May he convert to the doctrine the hearts of the multitude
   assembled here.

Life is like a transient water-bubble,
and the longing of the heart for a teacher endures not.
Indolence is like the robbing of an empty house;
know ye not to turn away from emptiness?
Youth is like a summer flower;
will it not wither and die unheralded?
Old age is like fire catching a timber;
know ye not that it will reach its heart?
Birth and death are like the rising and setting of the sun;
they will be again and again, says the Buddha.
Sickness is like a young bird struck by a storm;
know ye not that the vigour of strength will be consumed?
Life is like a lamp fed upon oil;
verily it shall not abide eternally.
Evil is like a waterfall in a ravine;
I have never seen it turn back uphill.
The wicked man is like a poisonous stem;
whosoever clings thereto is lost.
Neglect of duty is like a pea nipped by frost;
whosoever leaves undone what he should have done is brought
   to naught.

*Practice of the faith is like husbandry of a field;*
*whosoever pursues it energetically reaps benefit.*
*The teacher is like honeyed medicine;*
*whosoever relies thereon is profited.*
*The solemn vow is like a watchman's tower;*
*whosoever keeps troth succeeds.*
*Good and bad actions are like the round of existence;*
*whosoever trespasses suffers therefrom.*
*The circle of transmigration is like an envenomed thorn;*
*whosoever runs into it is doomed.*
*Death is like a shadow cast by the sun;*
*I have never seen it prevented.*
*When the time for such things comes,*
*apart from the holy faith*
*there is none to afford protection.*
*The holy faith is from the Buddhas who have fulfilled it,*
*but there is now none to desire it.*
*Worldly marriage gives birth to evil actions*
*and evil actions bring greedy striving for birth.*
*He who is content to talk about the faith,*
*when faced with reality, is incontinently overwhelmed.*
*O almsgiver, increase not thine eloquence*
*but practise the holy faith.*

# Glossary

1   The six kinds of beings are gods, titans, men, animals, hungry ghosts and inhabitants of hell.

2   The ten virtues are (of the body) not to kill, not to take what is not given, to be pure in deed; (of speech) to speak the truth, to speak gently, to keep a promise, to avoid slander; (of the mind) not to covet another's goods, not to devise harm to another and to have right views.

3   The three powers of mind are contemplation, meditation and consummation.

4   The ritual of creation and perfection is the ceremony of conjuring up a divinity gentle or fierce and then re-absorbing him (see Preface).

5   The triple body is composed of the body of truth, the body of fruition and the body of manifestation.

6   The eight worldly principles are gain, loss, fame, ill-fame, praise, slander, happiness and unhappiness.

7   The eight impediments are rebirth as an inhabitant of hell, as an animal, as a hungry ghost, as a long-lived god, as a savage, as a person defective in mind or body, as a heretic, or in a place where the Buddha has not appeared.

8   The six doctrines of Naropa are the mastery of the inner heat (see Preface); the realization of the illusiveness of nature; the realization of the illusiveness of dreams; the beatific vision of the transcendent void; the guidance through the intermediate state between death and re-birth; and the art of the transference of the consciousness from body to body and place to place. (These are described in Book III of *Tibetan Yoga and Secret Doctrines*.)

9   The sevenfold wealth is clear memory, subtle comprehension of the teaching, pure endeavour, pure joy, pure meditation, pure rapture and experience of the transcendent void.

10   The triple refuge and jewel is the Buddha, the Doctrine and the Congregation.

11   The triple pain is that of body, speech and mind.

12   The three original bonds are desire, anger and ignorance.

13   The five-fold nectar is freedom from desire, patience, knowledge, long-suffering and humility.

14   The four immeasurable virtues are perfect art, perfect prayer, perfect fortitude and perfect enlightenment.

15   The three worlds are the world of desire, the world of forms and the world of the unmanifest.